I0430104

Overview: ESF and Support Annexes
Coordinating Federal Assistance
In Support of the National Response Framework

January 2008

Homeland
Security

This document was developed expressly for emergency management practitioners as an overview of the process, roles, and responsibilities for requesting and providing all forms of Federal assistance. This overview also presents a summary of each of the 15 Emergency Support Function Annexes and 8 Support Annexes including their purpose, capabilities, membership, and concept of operations. The complete annexes are contained in the online NRF Resource Center.

For further information on how the Nation conducts incident response, refer to the *National Response Framework*.

Intentionally Left Blank

CONTENTS

Intentionally Left Blank

INTRODUCTION

The *National Response Framework (NRF)* presents the guiding principles that enable all response partners to prepare for and provide a unified national response to disasters and emergencies – from the smallest incident to the largest catastrophe. The *Framework* defines the key principles, roles, and structures that organize the way we respond as a Nation. It describes how communities, tribes, States, the Federal Government, and private-sector and nongovernmental partners apply these principles for a coordinated, effective national response. The *National Response Framework* is always in effect, and elements can be implemented at any level at any time.

This Overview supports and provides additional guidance concerning the *Framework*. In particular, this document focuses on the essential processes for requesting and receiving Federal assistance and summarizes the key response capabilities and essential support elements provided through the Emergency Support Function (ESF) Annexes and Support Annexes.

The Overview includes the following topics:

1. **Key Players:** Organizations and entities that may either need assistance or provide assistance

2. **Federal Assistance:** Descriptions of the processes for requesting and obtaining Federal assistance in support of States, tribes, local jurisdictions, and other Federal partners

3. **Emergency Support Function Annexes:** Summaries of the 15 ESF Annexes, which group Federal resources and capabilities into functional areas to serve as the primary mechanisms for providing assistance at the operational level

4. **Support Annexes:** Summaries of the 8 Support Annexes, which describe essential supporting aspects that are common to all incidents

The *Framework* also includes Incident Annexes that address specific categories of contingencies or hazard situations requiring specialized application of *Framework* mechanisms. The Incident Annexes are not directly addressed or summarized in this support document. Readers should review the Incident Annexes on the NRF Resource Center, http://www.fema.gov/NRF.

Details relating to requesting and receiving assistance, as well as the authorities under which assistance is provided, are available on the NRF Resource Center. Response Partner Guides, information on Stafford Act and non-Stafford Act assistance, all annexes, and a listing of legal authorities are available on this Web site.

KEY PLAYERS

LOCAL GOVERNMENTS

Local governments (counties, cities, or towns) respond to emergencies daily using their own resources. They also rely on mutual aid and assistance agreements with neighboring jurisdictions when they need additional resources. The *National Incident Management System (NIMS)* provides information on mutual aid and assistance agreements.

When local jurisdictions cannot meet incident response resource needs with their own resources or with help available from other local jurisdictions, they may ask the State for assistance.

TRIBAL GOVERNMENTS

Tribal governments respond to the same range of emergencies and disasters that other jurisdictions face. They may require assistance from neighboring jurisdictions under mutual aid and assistance agreements and may provide assistance as well.

The United States has a trust relationship with Indian tribes and recognizes their right to self-government. As such, tribal governments are responsible for coordinating resources to address actual or potential incidents. When local resources are not adequate, tribal leaders seek assistance from States or the Federal Government.

For certain types of Federal assistance, tribal governments work with the State, but as sovereign entities they can also elect to deal directly with the Federal Government for other types of assistance. In order to obtain Federal assistance via the Robert T. Stafford Disaster Relief and Emergency Assistance Act (Stafford Act), the State Governor must request a Presidential declaration on behalf of a tribe.

STATE GOVERNMENTS

The State helps local governments if they need assistance. States have significant resources of their own, including emergency management and homeland security agencies, State police, health agencies, transportation agencies, incident management teams, specialized teams, and the National Guard.

If additional resources are required, the State may request assistance from other States through interstate mutual aid and assistance agreements such as the Emergency Management Assistance Compact (EMAC). Administered by the National Emergency Management Association, EMAC is a congressionally ratified organization that provides form and structure to the interstate mutual aid and assistance process.[1]

If an incident is beyond the local and State capabilities, the Governor can seek Federal assistance. The State will collaborate with the impacted communities and the Federal Government to provide the help needed.

---

[1] For more detail about EMAC, see http://www.emacweb.org/.

KEY PLAYERS

FEDERAL GOVERNMENT

The Federal Government maintains a wide array of capabilities and resources that can assist State governments in responding to incidents. Federal departments and agencies provide this assistance using processes outlined later in this document. In addition, Federal departments and agencies may also request and receive help from other Federal departments and agencies.

NONGOVERNMENTAL ORGANIZATIONS

Nongovernmental and voluntary organizations are essential partners in responding to incidents. Working through emergency operations centers and other structures, nongovernmental and voluntary organizations assist local, tribal, State, and Federal governments in providing sheltering, emergency food supplies, counseling services, and other vital support services to support response and promote the recovery of disaster victims. These groups often provide specialized services that help individuals with special needs, including those with disabilities.

To engage these key partners most effectively, local, tribal, State, and Federal governments coordinate with voluntary agencies, existing Voluntary Organizations Active in Disaster (VOADs), community and faith-based organizations, and other entities to develop plans to manage volunteer services and donated goods, establish appropriate roles and responsibilities, and train and exercise plans and procedures before an incident occurs.

PRIVATE SECTOR

Forming the foundation for the health of the Nation's economy, the private sector is a key partner in local, tribal, State, and Federal incident management activities. The private sector is responsible for most of the critical infrastructure and key resources in the Nation and thus may require assistance in the wake of a disaster or emergency. They also provide goods and services critical to the response and recovery process, either on a paid basis or through donations.

FEDERAL ASSISTANCE

Federal disaster assistance is often thought of as synonymous with Presidential declarations and the Stafford Act. The fact is that Federal assistance can be provided to State, tribal, and local jurisdictions, and to other Federal departments and agencies, in a number of different ways through various mechanisms and authorities. Federal assistance does not always require coordination by the Department of Homeland Security (DHS) and may be provided without a Presidential major disaster or emergency declaration.

Federal assistance for incidents that do not require DHS coordination may be led by other Federal departments and agencies consistent with their authorities. The Secretary of Homeland Security may monitor such incidents and may activate *Framework* mechanisms to provide support to departments and agencies without assuming overall leadership for the Federal response to the incident.

FEDERAL SUPPORT TO STATES

STAFFORD ACT

Federal support to States and local jurisdictions takes many forms. The most widely known authority under which assistance is provided for major incidents is the Stafford Act.

When an incident occurs that exceeds or is anticipated to exceed local, tribal, or State resources, the Governor can request Federal assistance under the Stafford Act. The Stafford Act authorizes the President to provide financial and other assistance to State and local governments, certain private nonprofit organizations, and individuals to support response, recovery, and mitigation efforts following Presidential emergency or major disaster declarations.

Most incidents are not of sufficient magnitude to warrant a Presidential declaration. However, if State and local resources are insufficient, a Governor may ask the President to make such a declaration. Before making a declaration request, the Governor must activate the State's emergency plan and ensure that all appropriate State and local actions have been taken or initiated, including but not limited to:

- Surveying the affected areas to determine the extent of private and public damage.

- Conducting joint preliminary damage assessments with Federal Emergency Management Agency (FEMA) officials to estimate the types and extent of Federal disaster assistance required.

Ordinarily, only the Governor can initiate a request for a Presidential emergency or major disaster declaration. In extraordinary circumstances, the President may unilaterally make such a declaration. The Governor's request is made through the FEMA Regional Administrator and based on a finding that the disaster is of such severity and magnitude that effective response is beyond the capabilities of the State and affected local governments, and that Federal assistance is necessary.

FEDERAL ASSISTANCE

The Governor's request includes:

- Information on the extent and nature of State resources that have been or will be used to address the consequences of the disaster.

- A certification by the Governor that State and local governments will assume all applicable non-Federal costs required by the Stafford Act.

- An estimate of the types and amounts of supplementary Federal assistance required.

- Designation of the State Coordinating Officer.

The FEMA Regional Administrator evaluates the damage and requirements for Federal assistance and makes a recommendation to the FEMA Administrator. The FEMA Administrator, acting through the Secretary of Homeland Security, then recommends a course of action to the President. The Governor, appropriate Members of Congress, and Federal departments and agencies are immediately notified of a Presidential declaration.

Figure 1. Overview of Stafford Act Support to States

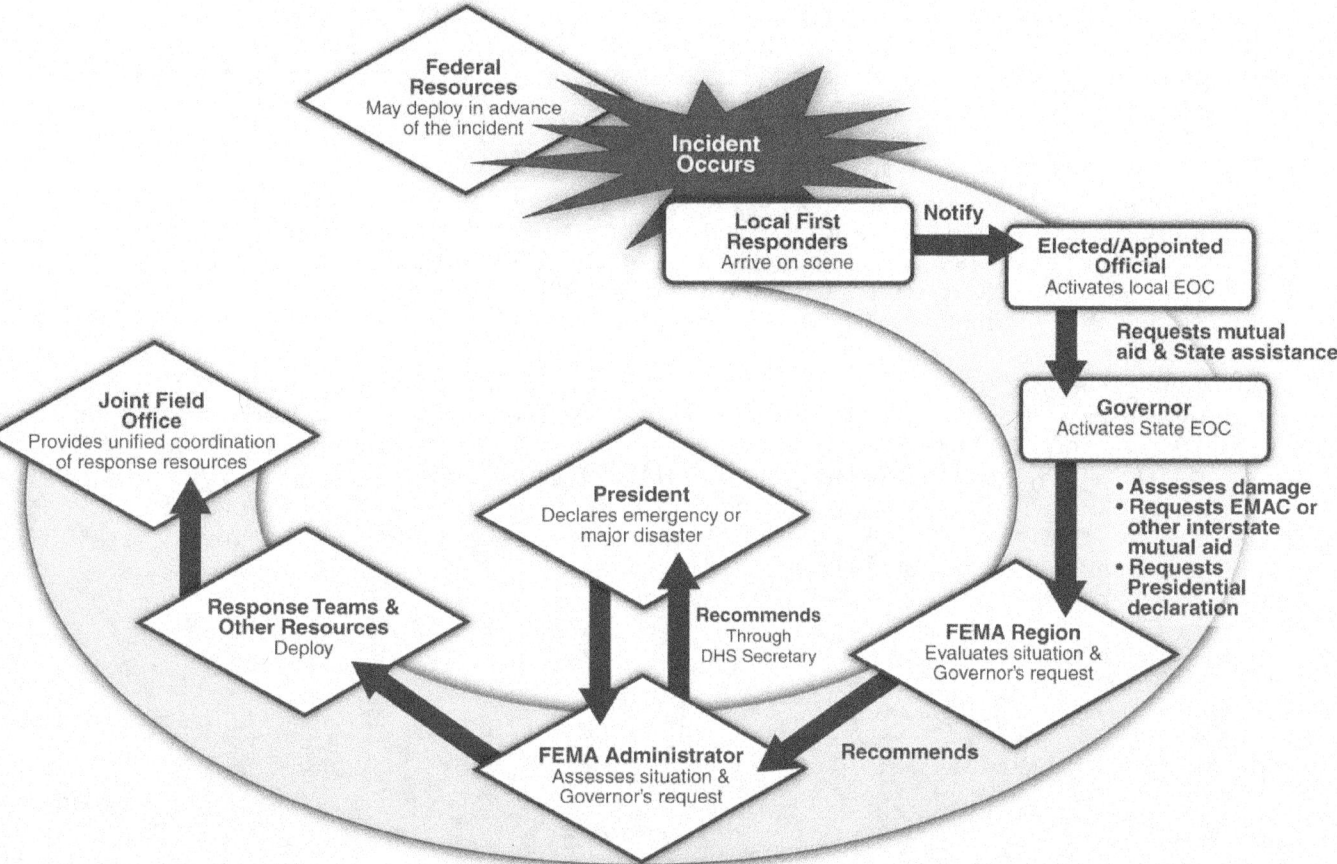

FEDERAL ASSISTANCE

NON-STAFFORD FEDERAL SUPPORT TO STATE AND LOCAL JURISDICTIONS

While the Stafford Act is the most familiar mechanism by which the Federal Government may provide support to State, tribal, and local governments, it is not the only one. Often, Federal assistance does not require coordination by DHS and can be provided without a Presidential major disaster or emergency declaration.

In these instances, Federal departments and agencies provide assistance to States, as well as directly to tribes and local jurisdictions, consistent with their own authorities. For example, under the Comprehensive Environmental Response, Compensation, and Liability Act, local and tribal governments can request assistance directly from the Environmental Protection Agency and/or the U.S. Coast Guard.

This support is typically coordinated by the Federal agency with primary jurisdiction rather than DHS. The Secretary of Homeland Security may monitor such incidents and may, as requested, activate *Framework* mechanisms to support Federal departments and agencies without assuming overall leadership for the incident.

NATIONAL DEFENSE AND DEFENSE SUPPORT OF CIVIL AUTHORITIES

The primary mission of the Department of Defense (DOD) and its components is national defense. Because of this critical role, resources are committed after approval by the Secretary of Defense or at the direction of the President. Many DOD components and agencies are authorized to respond to save lives, protect property and the environment, and mitigate human suffering under imminently serious conditions, as well as to provide support under their separate established authorities, as appropriate. The provision of defense support is evaluated by its legality, lethality, risk, cost, appropriateness, and impact on readiness. When Federal military and civilian personnel and resources are authorized to support civil authorities, command of those forces will remain with the Secretary of Defense. DOD elements in the incident area of operations and National Guard forces under the command of a Governor will coordinate closely with response organizations at all levels.

In rare circumstances, the President can federalize National Guard forces for domestic duties under Title 10 (e.g., in cases of invasion by a foreign nation, rebellion against the authority of the United States, or where the President is unable to execute the laws of the United States with regular forces (10 U.S.C. 12406)). When mobilized under Title 10 of the U.S. Code, the forces are no longer under the command of the Governor. Instead, DOD assumes full responsibility for all aspects of the deployment, including command and control over National Guard forces.

FEDERAL ASSISTANCE

FEDERAL LAW ENFORCEMENT ASSISTANCE

Each State has jurisdiction for enforcement of State laws, using State and local resources, including the National Guard (to the extent that the National Guard remains under State authority and has not been called into Federal service or ordered to active duty).

State governments may request Federal law enforcement assistance under the Emergency Federal Law Enforcement Assistance Act without a Presidential emergency or major disaster declaration. In addition, Federal agencies may request public safety and security or general law enforcement support from another Federal agency during a large-scale incident. The ESF #13 – Public Safety and Security Annex provides further guidance on the integration of public safety and security resources to support the full range of incident management functions.

FEDERAL-TO-FEDERAL SUPPORT

INTERAGENCY AGREEMENTS

Federal departments and agencies routinely manage the response to incidents under their statutory or executive authorities. For example, the Department of Agriculture/Forest Service and various agencies of the Department of the Interior conduct wildland firefighting activities under existing memorandums of agreement (MOAs) with other Federal, State, and local entities.

These types of responses do not require DHS coordination and are led by the Federal entity with primary jurisdiction. In these instances, the Secretary of Homeland Security may monitor such incidents and may, as requested, activate *Framework* mechanisms to provide support to departments and agencies without assuming overall leadership for the incident.

FEDERAL-TO-FEDERAL SUPPORT COORDINATED BY DHS

When a Federal entity with primary responsibility and authority for handling an incident requires Federal assistance above and beyond its interagency mechanisms (e.g., Executive orders, memorandums of understanding (MOUs), MOAs, etc.), that department or agency can request additional Federal assistance through DHS. When this happens, this support is:

- Coordinated by DHS using the multiagency coordination structures established in the *Framework* and in accordance with the *NIMS*.

- Generally funded by the Federal entity with primary responsibility and statutory authority for the incident in accordance with provisions of the Economy Act, unless other statutory authorities exist.

- Facilitated by the interagency MOU for Mutual Aid, and executed at the time of the incident through interagency agreements (see the Financial Management Support Annex for more information).

Intentionally Left Blank

EMERGENCY SUPPORT FUNCTION (ESF)
ANNEX SUMMARIES

Intentionally Left Blank

EMERGENCY SUPPORT FUNCTION ANNEXES: INTRODUCTION

The Federal Government and many State governments organize much of their resources and capabilities – as well as those of certain private-sector and nongovernmental organizations – under 15 Emergency Support Functions (ESFs). ESFs align categories of resources and provide strategic objectives for their use.

During a response, ESFs are a critical mechanism to coordinate functional capabilities and resources provided by Federal departments and agencies, along with certain private-sector and nongovernmental organizations. ESFs may be selectively activated for both Stafford Act and non-Stafford Act incidents where Federal departments or agencies request DHS assistance or under other circumstances as defined in Homeland Security Presidential Directive 5 (HSPD-5). Not all incidents result in the activation of ESFs.

ESFs may be activated to support headquarters, regional, and/or field activities. The Incident Command System provides for the flexibility to assign ESF and other stakeholder resources according to their capabilities, tasking, and requirements to augment and support the other sections of the Joint Field Office (JFO)/Regional Response Coordination Center (RRCC) or National Response Coordination Center (NRCC) in order to respond to incidents in a more collaborative and cross-cutting manner.

While ESFs are typically assigned to a specific section at the NRCC or in the JFO/RRCC for management purposes, resources may be assigned anywhere within the Unified Coordination structure. Regardless of the section in which an ESF may reside, that entity works in conjunction with other JFO sections to ensure that appropriate planning and execution of missions occur. For example, if a State requests assistance with a mass evacuation, the JFO would request personnel from ESF #1 (Transportation), ESF #6 (Mass Care, Emergency Assistance, Housing, and Human Services), and ESF #8 (Public Health and Medical Services). These would then be integrated into a single branch or group within the Operations Section to ensure effective coordination of evacuation services.

ESF MEMBER ROLES AND RESPONSIBILITIES

Each ESF Annex identifies the coordinator and the primary and support agencies pertinent to the ESF. Several ESFs incorporate multiple components, with primary agencies designated for each component to ensure seamless integration of and transition between preparedness, response, and recovery activities.

- **ESF Coordinator.** The ESF coordinator is the entity with management oversight for that particular ESF. The coordinator has ongoing responsibilities throughout the preparedness, response, and recovery phases of incident management. The role of the ESF coordinator is carried out through a "unified command" approach as agreed upon collectively by the designated primary agencies and, as appropriate, support agencies.

- **ESF Primary Agency(ies).** An ESF primary agency is a Federal agency with significant authorities, roles, resources, or capabilities for a particular function within an ESF. ESFs may have multiple primary agencies, and the specific responsibilities of those agencies are articulated within the relevant ESF Annex. A Federal agency designated as an ESF primary agency serves as a Federal executive agent under the Federal Coordinating Officer (or Federal Resource Coordinator for non-Stafford Act incidents) to accomplish the ESF mission

- **ESF Support Agencies.** Support agencies are those entities with specific capabilities or resources that support the primary agency(ies) in executing the mission of the ESF.

Intentionally Left Blank

ESF #1 – Transportation

Purpose

Emergency Support Function (ESF) #1 – Transportation provides support to the Department of Homeland Security (DHS) by assisting Federal, State, tribal, and local governmental entities, voluntary organizations, nongovernmental organizations, and the private sector in the management of transportation systems and infrastructure during domestic threats or in response to incidents. ESF #1 also participates in prevention, preparedness, response, recovery, and mitigation activities. ESF #1 carries out the Department of Transportation (DOT)'s statutory responsibilities, including regulation of transportation, management of the Nation's airspace, and ensuring the safety and security of the national transportation system.

Capabilities

ESF #1 embodies considerable intermodal expertise and public- and private-sector transportation stakeholder relationships. DOT, with the assistance of the ESF #1 support agencies, provides transportation assistance in domestic incident management, including the following activities:

- Monitor and report status of and damage to the transportation system and infrastructure as a result of the incident.

- Identify temporary alternative transportation solutions that can be implemented by others when systems or infrastructure are damaged, unavailable, or overwhelmed.

- Perform activities conducted under the direct authority of DOT elements as these relate to aviation, maritime, surface, railroad, and pipeline transportation.

- Coordinate the restoration and recovery of the transportation systems and infrastructure.

- Coordinate and support prevention, preparedness, response, recovery, and mitigation activities among transportation stakeholders within the authorities and resource limitations of ESF #1 agencies.

Members

ESF Coordinator: Department of Transportation (DOT)

Primary Agency: Department of Transportation (DOT)

Support Agencies:

- Department of Agriculture
- Department of Commerce
- Department of Defense
- Department of Energy
- Department of Homeland Security

- Department of the Interior
- Department of Justice
- Department of State
- General Services Administration
- U.S. Postal Service

ESF #1 – TRANSPORTATION

CONCEPT OF OPERATIONS OVERVIEW

ESF #1 provides DHS with a single point to obtain key transportation-related information, planning, and emergency management, including prevention, preparedness, response, recovery, and mitigation capabilities at the Headquarters, regional, State, and local levels. The ESF #1 structure integrates DOT and support agency capabilities and resources into the *National Response Framework* and the *National Incident Management System (NIMS)*.

The National Response Coordination Center (NRCC) issues operation orders and mission assignments to activate ESF #1 based on the scope and magnitude of the threat or incident. The NRCC notifies the DOT Crisis Management Center (CMC), which serves as the focal point for the Department's emergency response and the formal point of contact for ESF #1 activation within DOT.

Immediately upon notification of a threat or an imminent or actual incident, the following actions will be taken, as required:

- Initiate reporting to the Office of the Secretary of Transportation, the National Operations Center (NOC) elements, Domestic Readiness Group (DRG), Counterterrorism Security Group (CSG), DOT operating administrations and regional offices, and the Regional Emergency Transportation Coordinator (RETCO).

- Activate the DOT Emergency Response Team, if required.

- Staff ESF #1 at the NRCC.

- Dispatch staff to the Incident Management Planning Team (IMPT), DRG, CSG, NRCC, RRCC(s), Joint Field Office(s), and Evacuation Liaison Team.

- Activate the Regional Emergency Transportation Coordinator and Representatives (RETCO/RETREPs).

- Inform and invite participation by ESF #1 support agencies, as needed.

Initial response activities that ESF #1 conducts during emergencies include the following:

- Monitoring and reporting the status of and damage to the transportation system and infrastructure.

- Identifying temporary alternative transportation solutions to be implemented by others when primary systems or routes are unavailable or overwhelmed.

- Implementing appropriate air traffic and airspace management measures.

- Coordinating the issuance of regulatory waivers and exemptions.

To see the complete annex, as well as other pertinent information, refer to the NRF Resource Center at www.fema.gov/NRF.

ESF #2 – COMMUNICATIONS

PURPOSE

Emergency Support Function (ESF) #2 – Communications supports the restoration of the communications infrastructure, facilitates the recovery of systems and applications from cyber attacks, and coordinates Federal communications support to response efforts during incidents requiring a coordinated Federal response. This ESF implements the provisions of the Office of Science and Technology Policy (OSTP) National Plan for Telecommunications Support in Non-Wartime Emergencies (NPTS).

ESF #2 also provides communications support to Federal, State, tribal, and local governments and first responders when their systems have been impacted, and provides communications and information technology (IT) support to the Joint Field Office (JFO) and JFO field teams.

With the rapid convergence of communications and IT, the National Communications System (NCS) and the National Cyber Security Division (NCSD) work closely to coordinate the ESF #2 response to cyber incidents. This convergence requires increased synchronization of effort and capabilities between the communications and IT sectors to facilitate ESF #2's ability to respond to all types of incidents.

CAPABILITIES

ESF #2:

- Coordinates Federal actions to assist industry in restoring the public communications infrastructure and to assist State, tribal, and local governments with emergency communications and restoration of public safety communications systems and first responder networks.

- Supports Federal departments and agencies in procuring and coordinating National Security and Emergency Preparedness (NS/EP) communications services.

- Provides communications support to the JFO and any JFO field teams.

- Addresses cyber security issues that result from or occur in conjunction with incidents. However, for incidents that are primarily cyber in nature, the Cyber Incident Annex is used and ESF #2 supports responses to cyber incidents as directed.

MEMBERS

ESF Coordinator: Department of Homeland Security (DHS)/National Protection and Programs/Cybersecurity and Communications/National Communications System

Primary Agencies:
Department of Homeland Security (DHS)/National Protection and Programs/Cybersecurity and Communications/National Communications System
Department of Homeland Security (DHS)/Federal Emergency Management Agency (FEMA)

ESF #2 – COMMUNICATIONS

Support Agencies:

- Department of Agriculture/Forest Service
- Department of Commerce
- Department of Defense
- Department of Homeland Security

- Department of the Interior
- Federal Communications Commission
- General Services Administration

DHS/FEMA activates ESF #2 when a significant impact to the communications infrastructure is expected or has occurred. When activated, ESF #2 provides communications support to the impacted area, as well as internally to the JFO and associated Federal JFO teams. ESF #2 support is scalable to meet the specific needs of each incident response, and response resources are drawn from a matrix of personnel and equipment available from the ESF #2 support agencies.

CONCEPT OF OPERATIONS OVERVIEW

NCS:

- Acts as the ESF #2 primary agency in accordance with the Memorandum from OSTP to the Manager, NCS, dated June 11, 1993, to include exercising primary responsibility for restoration of telecommunications in an incident area.
- Coordinates the planning for and provision of NS/EP communications for the Federal Government under all circumstances, including crisis or emergency, attack, recovery, and reconstitution, in accordance with Executive Order 12472.
- Designates an FECC to lead ESF #2 when it is activated.
- Designates a team lead for a component responsible for communications infrastructure restoration functions.
- Coordinates the restoration of communications infrastructure and supports Federal departments and agencies in procuring and coordinating NS/EP communications services when the component responsible for communications infrastructure restoration functions becomes operational.

FEMA:

- Provides short-term restoration support to State, tribal, and local government emergency communications in the event of a failure.
- Designates a team lead for a component responsible for tactical communications functions and personnel to support tactical communications functions.
- Coordinates with NCS and support agencies to develop appropriate documentation, policies, and procedures pertinent to tactical communications functions.
- Provides communications support to State, tribal, and local first responders.
- Coordinates the restoration of public safety communications systems and first responder networks.
- Provides communications and information technology support to the JFO, JFO field teams, and other Federal response/recovery facilities within the area of operation.

To see the complete annex, as well as other pertinent information, refer to the NRF Resource Center at www.fema.gov/NRF.

ESF #3 – PUBLIC WORKS AND ENGINEERING

PURPOSE

Emergency Support Function (ESF) #3 – Public Works and Engineering assists the Department of Homeland Security (DHS) by coordinating and organizing the capabilities and resources of the Federal Government to facilitate the delivery of services, technical assistance, engineering expertise, construction management, and other support to prepare for, respond to, and/or recover from a disaster or an incident requiring a coordinated Federal response.

CAPABILITIES

ESF #3 is structured to provide public works and engineering-related support for the changing requirements of domestic incident management to include preparedness, response, and recovery actions.

Activities include:

- Conducting preincident and postincident assessments of public works and infrastructure.

- Executing emergency contract support for life-saving and life-sustaining services.

- Providing technical assistance to include engineering expertise, construction management, and contracting and real estate services.

- Providing emergency repair of damaged public infrastructure and critical facilities.

- Implementing and managing the DHS/Federal Emergency Management Agency (FEMA) Public Assistance Program and other recovery programs.

MEMBERS

ESF Coordinator: Department of Defense (DOD)/U.S. Army Corps of Engineers

Primary Agencies:
Department of Defense (DOD)/U.S. Army Corps of Engineers
Department of Homeland Security (DHS)/Federal Emergency Management Agency (FEMA)

Support Agencies:

- Department of Agriculture
- Department of Commerce
- Department of Defense
- Department of Energy
- Department of Health and Human Services
- Department of Homeland Security
- Department of the Interior
- Department of Labor
- Department of State

- Department of Transportation
- Department of Veterans Affairs
- Environmental Protection Agency
- General Services Administration
- Nuclear Regulatory Commission
- Tennessee Valley Authority
- American Red Cross
- Corporation for National and Community Service

ESF #3 – PUBLIC WORKS AND ENGINEERING

CONCEPT OF OPERATIONS OVERVIEW

The Department of Defense (DOD)/U.S. Army Corps of Engineers (USACE) is the primary agency for providing ESF #3 technical assistance, engineering, and construction management resources and support during response activities.

DHS/FEMA is the primary agency for providing ESF #3 recovery resources and support, to include assistance under the DHS/FEMA Stafford Act Public Assistance Program. The Public Assistance Program provides supplemental Federal disaster grant assistance for debris removal and disposal; emergency protective measures; and the repair, replacement, or restoration of disaster-damaged public facilities and the facilities of certain qualified private nonprofit organizations.

Close coordination is maintained with Federal, State, tribal, and local officials to determine potential needs for support and to track the status of response and recovery activities.

Priorities are determined jointly among State, tribal, and/or local officials. Federal ESF #3 support is integrated into the overall Federal, State, tribal, local, nongovernmental organization (NGO), and private-sector efforts.

Support agency representatives collocate with ESF #3 field personnel to coordinate support as necessary.

To see the complete annex, as well as other pertinent information, refer to the NRF Resource Center at www.fema.gov/NRF.

ESF #4 – FIREFIGHTING

PURPOSE

Emergency Support Function (ESF) #4 – Firefighting provides Federal support for the detection and suppression of wildland, rural, and urban fires resulting from, or occurring coincidentally with, an incident requiring a coordinated Federal response for assistance.

CAPABILITIES

ESF #4 manages and coordinates firefighting activities, including:

- Detecting and suppressing fires on Federal lands.

- Providing personnel, equipment, and supplies in support of State, tribal, and local agencies involved in rural and urban firefighting operations.

MEMBERS

ESF Coordinator: Department of Agriculture/Forest Service

Primary Agency: Department of Agriculture/Forest Service

Support Agencies:
- Department of Commerce
- Department of Defense
- Department of Homeland Security
- Department of the Interior
- Department of State
- Environmental Protection Agency

CONCEPT OF OPERATIONS OVERVIEW

ESF #4 uses established firefighting and support organizations, processes, and procedures of *the National Incident Management System (NIMS)* as outlined in the *National Interagency Mobilization Guide*. Responsibility for situation assessment and determination of resource needs lies primarily with the local Incident Commander.

States have the option of requesting interstate and intrastate firefighting assistance and resources, both utilizing existing agreements. Intrastate resources would be requested under local or statewide mutual aid and assistance agreements. Interstate resources, including National Guard firefighting resources from other States, would be requested through the Emergency Management Assistance Compact (EMAC), other compacts, or State-to-State mutual aid and assistance agreements.

Requests for Federal assistance in obtaining firefighting resources for incidents other than wildland fires are transmitted from the Regional Response Coordination Center (RRCC) or Joint Field Office (JFO) ESF #4 representative to the appropriate Geographic Area Coordination Center (GACC). For wildland fire incidents, requests for assistance in obtaining firefighting resources are submitted as per the *National Interagency Mobilization Guide* to the GACC and coordinated with the JFO. For resources beyond those available within the geographic area, the requests are sent to the National Interagency Coordination Center (NICC) in Boise, ID, by the Geographical Area

Coordinator. The NICC contacts the national ESF #4 coordinator in the event of national-level shortages or unavailability of needed resources.

All Federal military personnel and resources for firefighting and incident management activities will be requested through the NICC in coordination with the Defense Coordinating Officer and the National Response Coordination Center.

Shortages of critical resources are adjudicated at the lowest jurisdictional level. If needed, resolution would begin at the JFO, then progress to the NRCC, and then to the Domestic Readiness Group (DRG).

Actual firefighting operations are managed under the Incident Command System element of the *NIMS* Command and Management component.

Situation and damage assessment information is transmitted through established channels and directly between the headquarters-level and regional-level functions according to *NIMS* procedures.

To see the complete annex, as well as other pertinent information, refer to the NRF Resource Center at www.fema.gov/NRF.

ESF #5 – Emergency Management

Purpose

Emergency Support Function (ESF) #5 – Emergency Management is responsible for supporting overall activities of the Federal Government for domestic incident management. ESF #5 provides the core management and administrative functions in support of National Response Coordination Center (NRCC), Regional Response Coordination Center (RRCC), and Joint Field Office (JFO) operations.

Capabilities

ESF #5 serves as the coordination ESF for all Federal departments and agencies across the spectrum of domestic incident management from hazard mitigation and preparedness to response and recovery.

ESF #5 preparedness activities include:

- Identifying resources for alert, activation, and subsequent deployment.

- Ensuring that there are trained and experienced staff to fill appropriate positions in the NRCC, RRCC, Initial Operating Facility, and JFO, when activated or established.

During the postincident response phase, ESF #5 is responsible for the support and planning functions. ESF #5 activities include those functions that are critical to support and facilitate multiagency planning and coordination, including:

- Alerts and notifications.

- Staffing and deploying of Department of Homeland Security (DHS) and DHS/Federal Emergency Management Agency (FEMA) response teams, as well as response teams from other Federal departments and agencies.

- Incident action planning.

- Coordination of operations, direction, and control.

- Logistics management.

- Information collection, analysis, and management.

- Facilitation of requests for Federal assistance.

- Resource acquisition and management.

- Federal worker safety and health.

- Facilities management.

- Financial management.

ESF #5 – EMERGENCY MANAGEMENT

MEMBERS

ESF Coordinator: Department of Homeland Security (DHS)/Federal Emergency Management Agency (FEMA)

Primary Agency: Department of Homeland Security (DHS)/Federal Emergency Management Agency (FEMA)

Support Agencies:

- Department of Agriculture
- Department of Commerce
- Department of Defense
- Department of Education
- Department of Energy
- Department of Health and Human Services
- Department of Homeland Security
- Department of Housing and Urban Development
- Department of the Interior
- Department of Justice
- Department of Labor
- Department of State
- Department of Transportation
- Department of the Treasury
- Department of Veterans Affairs
- Environmental Protection Agency
- Federal Communications Commission
- General Services Administration
- National Aeronautics and Space Administration
- Nuclear Regulatory Commission
- Office of Personnel Management
- Small Business Administration
- Tennessee Valley Authority
- U.S. Postal Service
- American Red Cross

CONCEPT OF OPERATIONS OVERVIEW

The NRCC, staffed by ESF #5 and other ESFs when activated, monitors potential or developing incidents and supports the efforts of regional and field operations. In the event of a no-notice event, the Secretary of Homeland Security or his or her designee may direct execution of the Catastrophic Incident Supplement depending of the size of the incident.

The RRCC, staffed by ESF #5 and other ESFs as required, coordinates operations and situational reporting to the NRCC until the JFO is operational. Once the JFO is operational, the RRCC assumes a monitoring role.

ESF #5 operations transition from the RRCC to the JFO when the JFO is established. When the JFO begins to stand-down operations, ESF #5 operations transition back to the RRCC, as required.

To see the complete annex, as well as other pertinent information, refer to the NRF Resource Center at www.fema.gov/NRF.

ESF #6 – MASS CARE, EMERGENCY ASSISTANCE, HOUSING, AND HUMAN SERVICES

PURPOSE

Emergency Support Function (ESF) #6 – Mass Care, Emergency Assistance, Housing, and Human Services coordinates the delivery of Federal mass care, emergency assistance, housing, and human services when local, tribal, and State response and recovery needs exceed their capabilities.

CAPABILITIES

ESF #6 is organized into the following four primary functions:

- **Mass Care:** Includes sheltering, feeding operations, emergency first aid, bulk distribution of emergency items, and collecting and providing information on victims to family members.

- **Emergency Assistance:** Assistance required by individuals, families, and their communities to ensure that immediate needs beyond the scope of the traditional "mass care" services provided at the local level are addressed. These services include: support to evacuations (including registration and tracking of evacuees); reunification of families; provision of aid and services to special needs populations; evacuation, sheltering, and other emergency services for household pets and services animals; support to specialized shelters; support to medical shelters; nonconventional shelter management; coordination of donated goods and services; and coordination of voluntary agency assistance.

- **Housing:** Includes housing options such as rental assistance, repair, loan assistance, replacement, factory-built housing, semipermanent and permanent construction, referrals, identification and provision of accessible housing, and access to other sources of housing assistance. This assistance is guided by the National Disaster Housing Strategy.

- **Human Services:** Includes the implementation of disaster assistance programs to help disaster victims recover their nonhousing losses, including programs to replace destroyed personal property, and help to obtain disaster loans, food stamps, crisis counseling, disaster unemployment, disaster legal services, support and services for special needs populations, and other Federal and State benefits.

MEMBERS

ESF Coordinator: Department of Homeland Security (DHS)/Federal Emergency Management Agency (FEMA)

Primary Agency: Department of Homeland Security (DHS)/Federal Emergency Management Agency (FEMA)

ESF #6 – MASS CARE, EMERGENCY ASSISTANCE, HOUSING, AND HUMAN SERVICES

Support Agencies:

- Department of Agriculture
- Department of Defense
- Department of Health and Human Services
- Department of Homeland Security
- Department of Housing and Urban Development
- Department of the Interior
- Department of Justice
- Department of Labor
- Department of Transportation
- Department of the Treasury
- Department of Veterans Affairs

- General Services Administration
- Small Business Administration
- Social Security Administration
- U.S. Postal Service
- American Red Cross
- Corporation for National and Community Service
- National Voluntary Organizations Active in Disaster
- Other voluntary agency and nongovernmental support organizations

CONCEPT OF OPERATIONS OVERVIEW

DHS/FEMA will coordinate Federal response and recovery operations in close coordination with local, tribal, and State governments, voluntary agencies (VOLAGs), and the private sector.

ESF #6 assistance is managed and coordinated at the lowest possible organizational level—e.g., the Joint Field Office (JFO) and the Regional Response Coordination Center (RRCC).

Only requests that cannot be filled or issues that cannot be resolved at the RRCC/JFO levels are elevated to the National Response Coordination Center (NRCC) ESF #6 Branch for resolution.

Initial response activities will focus on immediate needs of victims.

To see the complete annex, as well as other pertinent information, refer to the NRF Resource Center at www.fema.gov/NRF.

ESF #7 – LOGISTICS MANAGEMENT AND RESOURCE SUPPORT

PURPOSE

Emergency Support Function (ESF) #7 – Logistics Management and Resource Support assists the Department of Homeland Security (DHS) in providing a comprehensive, national disaster logistics planning, management, and sustainment capability that harnesses the resources of Federal logistics partners, key public and private stakeholders, and nongovernmental organizations (NGOs) to meet the needs of disaster victims and responders.

CAPABILITIES

ESF #7 provides logistics management and resource support to Federal, State, tribal, and local governments. The General Services Administration (GSA) and DHS/Federal Emergency Management Agency (FEMA) provide support which consists of:

- GSA providing: emergency relief supplies; facility space; office equipment; office supplies; telecommunications (in accordance with the Office of Science and Technology Policy National Plan for Telecommunications Support in Non-Wartime Emergencies); contracting services; transportation services; personnel required to support immediate response activities; and support for requirements not specifically identified in other ESFs, including excess and surplus property.

- DHS/FEMA Logistics providing a nationally integrated process for the collaborative implementation of the logistics capability of Federal agencies, public- and private-sector partners, and nongovernmental organizations.

MEMBERS

ESF Coordinators: General Services Administration (GSA)
Department of Homeland Security (DHS)/Federal Emergency Management Agency (FEMA)

Primary Agencies:
General Services Administration (GSA)
Department of Homeland Security (DHS)/Federal Emergency Management Agency (FEMA)

Support Agencies:

- Department of Agriculture
- Department of Commerce
- Department of Defense
- Department of Energy
- Department of Health and Human Services
- Department of Homeland Security

- Department of the Interior
- Department of Labor
- Department of Transportation
- Department of Veterans Affairs
- National Aeronautics and Space Administration
- Office of Personnel Management

ESF #7 – LOGISTICS MANAGEMENT AND RESOURCE SUPPORT

CONCEPT OF OPERATIONS OVERVIEW

GSA activities are conducted primarily within the various organizational elements detailed in the *National Response Framework* core document.

The DHS/FEMA Logistics adaptation of a supply chain management approach to managing the national logistics processes focuses the efforts of all partners and stakeholders of the end-to-end supply chain processes, beginning with planning of customer-driven requirements for materiel and services, delivery to disaster victims as requested by the State or tribe, and ending with replenishment of agency inventories.

Supply chain planning occurs at all levels within the national logistics management process. Strategic planning occurs within FEMA's Logistics Management Directorate supported by the following GSA elements: the Office of Emergency Response and Recovery, Public Building Service (PBS), and Federal Acquisition Service (FAS).

The headquarters- and regional-level Logistics Management Structures are managed by DHS/FEMA.

The headquarters-level Resource Support Structure is operated under the direction of the GSA Emergency Coordinator (EC) while the regional-level Resource Support Structure is operated under the direction of the GSA Regional Administrator (RA), Regional Emergency Coordinator (REC), or Deputy REC (DREC).

In the field, DHS/FEMA and GSA will provide staff to support the ESF #7 mission and the Logistics Section in the Joint Field Offices, Regional Response Coordination Centers, National Response Coordination Center, Federal Mobilization Centers (MOB Centers), and National Logistics Staging Areas for management and accountability of Federal supplies and equipment; resource ordering; delivery of equipment, supplies, and services; resource tracking; facility location and operations; transportation coordination; and management and support of information technology systems services and other administrative services.

The primary determination of supply and service requirements is made by operational elements at the regional level working in concert with the affected State. Requests for resources flow upward and are tracked at the headquarters level. Existing Federal resources provide the primary source of personnel, equipment, materials, and supplies. Support that cannot be provided from Federal resources is secured through direct procurement or donations.

Upon notification of an incident requiring a coordinated Federal response, the GSA EC makes an initial determination of which ESF #7 support agencies are required to provide immediate support and which are required to remain on standby.

To see the complete annex, as well as other pertinent information, refer to the NRF Resource Center at www.fema.gov/NRF.

ESF #8 – Public Health and Medical Services

Purpose

Emergency Support Function (ESF) #8 – Public Health and Medical Services provides the mechanism for coordinated Federal assistance to supplement State, tribal, and local resources in response to a public health and medical disaster, potential or actual incidents requiring a coordinated Federal response, and/or during a developing potential health and medical emergency. Public Health and Medical Services include responding to medical needs associated with mental health, behavioral health, and substance abuse considerations of incident victims and response workers. Services also cover the medical needs of members of the "at risk" or "special needs" population described in the Pandemic and All-Hazards Preparedness Act and in the *National Response Framework (NRF)* Glossary, respectively. It includes a population whose members may have medical and other functional needs before, during, and after an incident.

Capabilities

Public Health and Medical Services includes behavioral health needs consisting of both mental health and substance abuse considerations for incident victims and response workers and, as appropriate, medical needs groups defined in the core document as individuals in need of additional medical response assistance, and veterinary and/or animal health issues.

ESF #8 provides supplemental assistance to State, tribal, and local governments in the following core functional areas:

- Assessment of public health/medical needs
- Health surveillance
- Medical care personnel
- Health/medical/veterinary equipment and supplies
- Patient evacuation
- Patient care
- Safety and security of drugs, biologics, and medical devices
- Blood and blood products
- Food safety and security
- Agriculture safety and security
- All-hazard public health and medical consultation, technical assistance, and support
- Behavioral health care
- Public health and medical information
- Vector control
- Potable water/wastewater and solid waste disposal
- Mass fatality management, victim identification, and decontaminating remains
- Veterinary medical support

ESF #8 – Public Health and Medical Services

Members

ESF Coordinator: Department of Health and Human Services (HHS)

Primary Agency: Department of Health and Human Services (HHS)

Support Agencies:

- Department of Agriculture
- Department of Defense
- Department of Energy
- Department of Homeland Security
- Department of the Interior
- Department of Justice
- Department of Labor
- Department of State

- Department of Transportation
- Department of Veterans Affairs
- Environmental Protection Agency
- General Services Administration
- U.S. Agency for International Development
- U.S. Postal Service
- American Red Cross

Concept of Operations Overview

The Secretary of HHS leads the ESF #8 response. ESF #8, when activated, is coordinated by the Assistant Secretary for Preparedness and Response (ASPR). Once activated, ESF #8 functions are coordinated by the Emergency Management Group (EMG) through the Secretary's Operations Center. During the initial activation, HHS coordinates audio and video conference calls with the ESF #8 supporting departments and agencies, and public health and medical representatives from State, tribal, and local officials, to discuss the situation and determine the appropriate initial response actions.

HHS alerts and requests supporting organizations to provide a representative to the EMG to provide liaison support.

HHS may designate a Senior Health Official to serve as the senior Federal health official in the Joint Field Office (JFO).

Regional ESF #8 staff are ready to rapidly deploy, as the Incident Response Coordination Team – Advance (IRCT-A), to provide initial ESF #8 support to the affected location. As the situation matures, the IRCT-A will receive augmentation from HHS and partner agencies transitioning into a full IRCT capable of providing the full range of ESF #8 support to include medical command and control.

The regional ESF #8 staff includes representatives to staff the Regional Response Coordination Center and/or JFO, as required, on a 24-hour basis for the duration of the incident

---

To see the complete annex, as well as other pertinent information, refer to the NRF Resource Center at www.fema.gov/NRF.

ESF #9 – SEARCH AND RESCUE

PURPOSE

Emergency Support Function (ESF) #9 – Search and Rescue rapidly deploys components of the Federal Search and Rescue (SAR) Response System to provide specialized lifesaving assistance to State, tribal, and local authorities when activated for incidents or potential incidents requiring a coordinated Federal response.

CAPABILITIES

Search and rescue capabilities include distress monitoring, communications, location of distressed personnel, coordination, and execution of rescue operations including extrication or evacuation along with the provisioning of medical assistance and civilian services through the use of public and private resources to assist persons and property in potential or actual distress.

ESF #9 provides the following specialized SAR services during incidents or potential incidents requiring a coordinated Federal response:

- Structure Collapse (Urban) Search and Rescue (US&R)
- Waterborne Search and Rescue
- Inland/Wilderness Search and Rescue
- Aeronautical Search and Rescue

MEMBERS

ESF Coordinator: Department of Homeland Security (DHS)/Federal Emergency Management Agency (FEMA)

Primary Agencies:
Department of Homeland Security (DHS)/ Federal Emergency Management Agency (FEMA)
Department of Homeland Security (DHS)/U.S. Coast Guard (USCG)
Department of the Interior (DOI)/National Park Service (NPS)
Department of Defense (DOD)

Support Agencies:

- Department of Agriculture
- Department of Commerce
- Department of Defense
- Department of Health and Human Services
- Department of Homeland Security

- Department of Justice
- Department of Labor
- National Aeronautical and Space Administration
- U.S. Agency for International Development

ESF #9 – SEARCH AND RESCUE

CONCEPT OF OPERATIONS OVERVIEW

Immediate SAR operations are conducted in accordance with the National Search and Rescue Plan (NSP) and the U.S. National Search and Rescue Supplement (NSS) to the International Aeronautical and Maritime Search and Rescue Manual, which defines SAR responsibilities and provides guidance to the Federal agencies with civil SAR mandates.

Federal SAR response assists and augments State and local SAR capabilities in incidents requiring a coordinated Federal response or in accordance with the NSP, which defines the responsibilities and provides guidance to Federal agencies with civil SAR mandates.

Activation is dependent upon the nature and magnitude of the event, the suddenness of onset, and the existence of SAR resources in the affected area.

DHS/FEMA initiates the National Urban Search and Rescue (US&R) Response System for incidents requiring a coordinated Federal response that are likely to involve collapsed structures. The ESF #9 construct follows the National US&R Response System, which consists of US&R Task Forces, Incident Support Teams, and technical specialists as defined in the Urban Search and Rescue Operations System Description.

DHS/USCG initiates Federal waterborne SAR response activities for incidents requiring a coordinated Federal response that are likely to result in waterborne or maritime distress. The ESF #9 construct follows the SAR response structure outlined in the NSP, NSS, and the U.S. Coast Guard Addendum to the NSS. DHS/USCG coordinates ESF #9 response from an agency-designated command center (Area/District/Sector) or the nearest DHS/USCG Rescue Coordination Center (RCC), Rescue Sub-Center (RSC), or Joint Rescue Coordination Center (JRCC) to the affected area.

DOI/NPS initiates Federal SAR response activities for incidents requiring a coordinated Federal response that are likely to result in a distress situation in inland/wilderness areas. The ESF #9 construct reflects the SAR response structure as outlined in the NSP and NSS and other relevant DOI SAR procedures and SAR manuals. DOI coordinates ESF #9 response from one of its regional offices.

DOD/U.S. Air Force (USAF)/Air Force Rescue Coordination Center (AFRCC) initiates DOD SAR response operations conducted in aviation-related incidents. The ESF #9 construct follows the SAR response structure as outlined in the NSP, NSS, and the Air Force Rescue Coordination Center Operations Instructions. DOD/USAF/AFRCC coordinates initial activities from its Rescue Coordination Center. If significant DOD resources are required and/or a Joint Task Force (JTF) is activated, the AFRCC coordinates DOD response with the JTF.

To see the complete annex, as well as other pertinent information, refer to the NRF Resource Center at www.fema.gov/NRF.

ESF #10 – Oil and Hazardous Materials Response

Purpose

Emergency Support Function (ESF) #10 – Oil and Hazardous Materials Response provides Federal support in response to an actual or potential discharge and/or uncontrolled release of oil or hazardous materials when activated. ESF #10 provides for a coordinated Federal response to actual or potential oil and hazardous materials incidents.

Capabilities

The scope of ESF #10 includes the appropriate actions to prepare for, respond to, and recover from a threat to public health, welfare, or the environment caused by actual or potential oil and hazardous materials incidents. Appropriate general actions can include, but are not limited to efforts to:

- Prevent, minimize, or mitigate a release.
- Detect and assess the extent of contamination (including sampling and analysis and environmental monitoring).
- Stabilize the release and prevent the spread of contamination.
- Analyze options for environmental cleanup and waste disposition.
- Implement environmental cleanup.
- Store, treat, and dispose of oil and hazardous materials.

Examples of specific actions include:

- Sampling a drinking water supply to determine if there has been intentional contamination.
- Stabilizing the release through the use of berms, dikes, or impoundments.
- Capping of contaminated soils or sludge.
- Decontaminating buildings and structures.
- Using drainage controls, fences, warning signs, or other security or site-control precautions.
- Removing highly contaminated soils from drainage areas.

For a chemical, biological, or radiological Weapons of Mass Destruction (WMD) incident, ESF #10 may also provide, as needed, a Technical Specialist(s) to provide scientific and technical expertise and to coordinate scientific and technical issues with other responding agencies and with other ESF #10 headquarters, regional, and on-scene response elements.

Members

ESF Coordinator: Environmental Protection Agency (EPA)

Primary Agencies:
Environmental Protection Agency (EPA)
Department of Homeland Security (DHS)/U.S. Coast Guard (USCG)

ESF #10 – Oil and Hazardous Materials Response

Support Agencies:

- Department of Agriculture
- Department of Commerce
- Department of Defense
- Department of Energy
- Department of Health and Human Services
- Department of Homeland Security

- Department of the Interior
- Department of Justice
- Department of Labor
- Department of State
- Department of Transportation
- General Services Administration
- Nuclear Regulatory Commission

Concept of Operations Overview

For incidents where EPA is a primary agency, the Director, Office of Emergency Management, Office of Solid Waste and Emergency Response, EPA, serves as the lead for ESF #10.

For incidents where DHS/USCG is the primary agency, the Chief, Office of Incident Management and Preparedness, DHS/USCG, serves as the lead for ESF #10.

At the JFO level, ESF #10 typically provides a representative(s) to coordinate ESF #10 mission assignments and provide information to the JFO on ESF #10 on-scene activities.

To see the complete annex, as well as other pertinent information, refer to the NRF Resource Center at www.fema.gov/NRF.

ESF #11 – Agriculture and Natural Resources

Purpose

Emergency Support Function (ESF) #11 – Agriculture and Natural Resources supports State, tribal, and local authorities and other Federal agency efforts to:

- Provide nutrition assistance.
- Control and eradicate, as appropriate, any outbreak of a highly contagious or economically devastating animal/zoonotic (i.e., transmitted between animals and people) disease or any outbreak of an economically devastating plant pest or disease.
- Ensure the safety and security of the commercial food supply.
- Protect natural and cultural resources and historic properties (NCH) resources.
- Provide for the safety and well-being of household pets during an emergency response or evacuation situation.

Capabilities

ESF #11 includes the following five primary functions:

1. **Providing nutrition assistance:** Includes working with State agencies to determine nutrition assistance needs, obtain appropriate food supplies, arrange for delivery of the supplies, and authorize the Disaster Food Stamp Program. These efforts are coordinated by the Department of Agriculture (USDA), Food and Nutrition Service (FNS).

2. **Responding to animal and plant diseases and pests:** Includes implementing an integrated Federal, State, tribal, and local response to an outbreak of a highly contagious or economically devastating animal/zoonotic disease, or an outbreak of a harmful or economically significant plant pest or disease. ESF #11 ensures, in coordination with ESF #8 – Public Health and Medical Services, that animal/veterinary issues in natural disasters are supported. These efforts are coordinated by USDA's Animal and Plant Health Inspection Service (APHIS).

3. **Ensuring the safety and security of the commercial food supply:** Includes the execution of routine food safety inspections and other services to ensure the safety of food products that enter commerce. This includes the inspection and verification of food safety aspects of slaughter and processing plants, products in distribution and retail sites, and import facilities at ports of entry; laboratory analysis of food samples; control of products suspected to be adulterated; plant closures; foodborne disease surveillance; and field investigations. These efforts are coordinated by USDA's Food Safety and Inspection Service (FSIS).

4. **Protecting NCH resources:** Includes appropriate response actions to preserve, conserve, rehabilitate, recover, and restore NCH resources. This includes providing postevent baseline assessments of damages and providing technical assistance and resources for assessing impacts of response and recovery activities to NCH resources. These efforts are coordinated by the Department of the Interior (DOI).

5. **Providing for the safety and well-being of household pets:** Supports the Department of Homeland Security (DHS)/Federal Emergency Management Agency (FEMA) together with ESF #6 – Mass Care, Emergency Assistance, Housing, and Human Services; ESF #8; ESF #9 – Search and Rescue; and ESF #14 – Long-Term

ESF #11 – Agriculture and Natural Resources

Community Recovery to ensure an integrated response that provides for the safety and well-being of household pets. The ESF #11 effort is coordinated by USDA/APHIS.

Members

ESF Coordinator: Department of Agriculture (USDA)

Primary Agencies:
Department of Agriculture (USDA)
Department of the Interior (DOI)

Support Agencies:

- Department of Agriculture
- Department of Commerce
- Department of Defense
- Department of Energy
- Department of Health and Human Services
- Department of Homeland Security
- Department of the Interior
- Department of Justice
- Department of Labor
- Department of State

- Department of Transportation
- Environmental Protection Agency
- General Services Administration
- National Archives and Records Administration
- U.S. Postal Service
- Advisory Council on Historic Preservation
- American Red Cross
- Heritage Emergency National Task Force

Concept of Operations Overview

Once ESF #11 is activated, the national response is coordinated by USDA at the National Response Coordination Center. The coordinator convenes a conference call with appropriate support agencies and non-Federal partners to assess the situation and determine appropriate actions. The agency then alerts supporting organizations and requests that they provide representation.

The headquarters ESF operates under the direction of the USDA coordinator. When the assistance needed involves NCH resources protection, DOI provides headquarters direction and coordination. When an incident requires assistance from more than one of the ESF #11 functions, USDA provides the overall direction.

At the regional level, ESF #11 operates under the direction of a USDA coordinator, who is determined based upon the assistance needed for the specific incident. When an incident requires assistance from more than one of the ESF #11 functions, USDA provides the regional point of contact within the Regional Response Coordination Center and represents ESF #11 in its dealings with the Unified Coordination Group. ESF #11 will have staff on duty at the Joint Field Office on a 24-hour basis, as needed for the duration of the emergency.

To see the complete annex, as well as other pertinent information, refer to the NRF Resource Center at www.fema.gov/NRF.

ESF #12 – ENERGY

PURPOSE

Emergency Support Function (ESF) #12 – Energy is intended to facilitate the restoration of damaged energy systems and components when activated by the Secretary of Homeland Security for incidents requiring a coordinated Federal response. Under Department of Energy (DOE) leadership, ESF #12 is an integral part of the larger DOE responsibility of maintaining continuous and reliable energy supplies for the United States through preventive measures and restoration and recovery actions.

The term "energy" includes producing, refining, transporting, generating, transmitting, conserving, building, distributing, maintaining, and controlling energy systems and system components. All energy systems are considered critical infrastructure.

CAPABILITIES

ESF #12 collects, evaluates, and shares information on energy system damage and estimations on the impact of energy system outages within affected areas. Additionally, it provides information concerning the energy restoration process such as projected schedules, percent completion of restoration, and geographic information on the restoration. ESF #12 facilitates the restoration of energy systems through legal authorities and waivers. ESF #12 also provides technical expertise to the utilities, conducts field assessments, and assists government and private-sector stakeholders to overcome challenges in restoring the energy system.

ESF #12 provides the appropriate supplemental Federal assistance and resources to enable restoration in a timely manner.

Collectively, the primary and support agencies that comprise ESF #12:

- Serve as the focal point within the Federal Government for receipt of information on actual or projected damage to energy supply and distribution systems and requirements for system design and operations, and on procedures for preparedness, restoration, recovery, and mitigation.

- Advise Federal, State, tribal, and local authorities on priorities for energy restoration, assistance, and supply.

- Assist industry, State, tribal, and local authorities with requests for emergency response actions as required to meet the Nation's energy demands.

- Assist Federal departments and agencies by locating fuel for transportation, communications, emergency operations, and national defense.

- Provide guidance on the conservation and efficient use of energy to Federal, State, tribal, and local governments and to the public.

- Provide assistance to Federal, State, tribal, and local authorities utilizing Department of Homeland Security (DHS)/Federal Emergency Management Agency (FEMA)-established communications systems.

ESF #12 – Energy

Members

ESF Coordinator: Department of Energy (DOE)

Primary Agency: Department of Energy (DOE)

Support Agencies:

- Department of Agriculture
- Department of Commerce
- Department of Defense
- Department of Homeland Security
- Department of the Interior
- Department of Labor

- Department of State
- Department of Transportation
- Environmental Protection Agency
- Nuclear Regulatory Commission
- Tennessee Valley Authority

Concept of Operations Overview

ESF #12 is coordinated through Headquarters DOE. ESF #12 is activated when DHS/FEMA notifies the 24-hour Headquarters DOE Emergency Operations Center.

When activated by DHS/FEMA, ESF #12:

- Provides representatives to the DHS National Operations Center, Domestic Readiness Group, and National Response Coordination Center.

- Deploys representatives to the Regional Response Coordination Center (RRCC). The ESF #12 Team Leader at the RRCC coordinates assignments, actions, and other support until the Joint Field Office (JFO) is established and mission-execution responsibilities are transferred to the JFO ESF #12 Team Leader. ESF #12 provides incident-related reports and information to ESF #5 – Emergency Management.

- Deploys as members of incident management teams or the Rapid Needs Assessment Team.

- Deploys personnel to the JFO.

To see the complete annex, as well as other pertinent information, refer to the NRF Resource Center at www.fema.gov/NRF.

ESF #13 – PUBLIC SAFETY AND SECURITY

PURPOSE

Emergency Support Function (ESF) #13 – Public Safety and Security integrates Federal public safety and security capabilities and resources to support the full range of incident management activities associated with potential or actual incidents requiring a coordinated Federal response.

CAPABILITIES

ESF #13 provides a mechanism for coordinating and providing Federal-to-Federal support; Federal support to State, tribal, and local authorities; and/or support to other ESFs, consisting of noninvestigative law enforcement, public safety, and security capabilities and resources during potential or actual incidents requiring a coordinated Federal response.

ESF #13 provides Federal public safety and security assistance to support preparedness, response, and recovery priorities in circumstances where local, tribal, or State resources are overwhelmed or are inadequate, or where a unique Federal capability is required. This may include, but is not limited to, the following activities, when appropriate:

- **Preincident Coordination:** Supporting incident management planning activities and preincident actions required to assist in the mitigation of threats and hazards. This includes developing operational and tactical public safety and security plans, conducting technical security and/or vulnerability assessments, and deploying Federal public safety and security resources in response to specific threats or potential incidents.

- **Technical Assistance:** Providing expertise and coordination for security planning efforts and conducting technical assessments (e.g., vulnerability assessments, risk analyses, surveillance sensor architecture, etc.).

- **Specialized Public Safety and Security Assessment:** Identifying the need for ESF #13 support and analyzing potential factors (e.g., mapping, modeling, and forecasting for crowd size, impact of weather, and other conditions) that may affect resource allocations and requisite actions affecting public safety and security.

- **General Law Enforcement Assistance:** Providing basic law enforcement assistance to Federal, State, tribal, and local agencies during incidents that require a coordinated Federal response. Such assistance may include conducting routine patrol functions and making arrests as circumstances may require. The ESF #13 Standard Operating Procedures describe those situations where deputization by another Federal law enforcement agency or by a State or local law enforcement agency may be necessary, and the process for such deputization.

- **Badging and Credentialing:** Assisting State, tribal, and local authorities in the establishment of consistent processes for issuing identification badges to emergency responders and other personnel needing access to places within a controlled area, and verifying emergency responder credentials.

- **Access Control:** Providing security forces to support State, tribal, and local efforts (or to secure sites under Federal jurisdiction) to control access to the incident site and critical facilities.

- **Site Security:** Providing security forces and establishing protective measures around the incident site, critical infrastructure, and/or critical facilities. ESF #13 responsibilities should not be confused with site-security responsibilities of the Office of Security of the Department of Homeland Security (DHS)/Federal Emergency Management Agency (FEMA), which is responsible for providing security for DHS/FEMA facilities, to include a Joint Field Office (JFO). DHS/FEMA may request ESF #13 assistance if DHS/FEMA resources are overwhelmed.

- **Traffic and Crowd Control:** Providing emergency protective services to address public safety and security requirements.

- **Force Protection:** Providing for the protection of emergency responders and other workers operating in a high-threat environment, and for the operational security of emergency response operations wherever they may occur.

- **Specialized Security Resources:** Providing specialized security assets such as traffic barriers; chemical, biological, radiological, nuclear, and high-yield explosives detection devices; canine units; law enforcement personal protective gear; etc.

MEMBERS

ESF Coordinator: Department of Justice (DOJ)

Primary Agency: Department of Justice (DOJ)

Support Agencies: All Executive Branch departments and agencies possessing a public safety and security capability

CONCEPT OF OPERATIONS OVERVIEW

ESF #13 is activated in situations requiring extensive public safety and security and where State, tribal, and local government resources are overwhelmed or are inadequate, or for Federal-to-Federal support or in preincident or postincident situations that require protective solutions or capabilities unique to the Federal Government.

When ESF #13 is activated, DOJ deploys on-call representative(s) to the National Response Coordination Center (NRCC).

DOJ assesses the need for ESF #13 resources and coordinates response assistance and support in close cooperation with regional and field ESF #13 elements.

ESF #13 may provide personnel to staff the National Operations Center, the NRCC, the Regional Response Coordination Center, the Incident Command Post, the JFO, the Joint Information Center, and operational centers established as described in the Terrorism Incident Law Enforcement and Investigation Annex, as circumstances may require.

To see the complete annex, as well as other pertinent information, refer to the NRF Resource Center at www.fema.gov/NRF.

ESF #14 – LONG-TERM COMMUNITY RECOVERY

PURPOSE

Emergency Support Function (ESF) #14 – Long-Term Community Recovery provides a mechanism for coordinating Federal support to State, tribal, regional, and local governments, nongovernmental organizations (NGOs), and the private sector to enable community recovery from the long-term consequences of extraordinary disasters.

ESF #14 accomplishes this by identifying and facilitating availability and use of sources of recovery funding, and providing technical assistance (such as impact analyses) for community recovery and recovery planning support.

CAPABILITIES

ESF #14 may be activated for incidents that require a coordinated Federal response to address significant long-term impacts (e.g., impacts on housing, government operations, agriculture, businesses, employment, community infrastructure, the environment, human health, and social services) to foster sustainable recovery.

ESF #14 provides the coordination mechanisms for the Federal Government to:

- Convene interagency recovery expertise to provide strategic guidance to long-term recovery efforts.
- Identify and address long-term recovery issues, including those that fall between existing mandates of agencies.
- Avoid duplication of assistance, coordinate program application processes and planning requirements to streamline assistance processes, and identify and coordinate resolution of policy and program issues.
- Identify programs and activities across the public, private, and nonprofit sectors that similarly support long-term recovery and promote coordination between them.
- Identify appropriate Federal programs and agencies to support implementation of comprehensive long-term community planning and identify gaps in available resources.
- Identify appropriate Federal programs and agencies to support and facilitate continuity of long-term recovery activities.
- Work with State, tribal, and local governments; NGOs; and private-sector organizations to support long-term recovery planning for highly impacted communities.
- Link recovery planning to sound risk reduction practices to encourage a more viable recovery.
- Strategically apply subject-matter expertise to help communities recover from disasters.

ESF #14 – Long-Term Community Recovery

Members

ESF Coordinator: Department of Homeland Security (DHS)/Federal Emergency Management Agency (FEMA)

Primary Agencies:
Department of Agriculture (USDA)
Department of Homeland Security (DHS)
Department of Housing and Urban Development (HUD)
Small Business Administration (SBA)

Support Agencies:

- Department of Commerce
- Department of Defense
- Department of Energy
- Department of Health and Human Services
- Department of the Interior
- Department of Labor
- Department of Transportation
- Department of the Treasury
- Environmental Protection Agency
- Corporation for National and Community Service
- Delta Regional Authority
- American Red Cross
- National Voluntary Organizations Active in Disaster

Concept of Operations Overview

ESF #14 provides representatives to the National Response Coordination Center as requested. Primary agencies are responsible for coordinating ESF #14 planning and recovery activities and strengthening the capabilities of ESF #14.

Regional and Field Operations: The ESF #14 coordinator and primary agencies meet to determine the need to activate ESF #14 elements when the incident is likely to require significant Federal long-term community recovery assistance. Support agencies also have the right to approach the ESF #14 coordinator to request ESF #14 activation.

ESF #14 typically organizes within the Operations Section of the Joint Field Office, but may support other Sections as required. Agency representation depends on the nature and severity of the incident.

To see the complete annex, as well as other pertinent information, refer to the NRF Resource Center at www.fema.gov/NRF.

ESF #15 – EXTERNAL AFFAIRS

PURPOSE

Emergency Support Function (ESF) #15 – External Affairs ensures that sufficient Federal assets are deployed to the field during incidents requiring a coordinated Federal response to provide accurate, coordinated, timely and accessible information to affected audiences, including governments, media, the private sector, and the local populace, including the special needs population.

CAPABILITIES

ESF #15 coordinates Federal actions to provide the required external affairs support to Federal, State, tribal, and local incident management elements.

Resources provided by the Department of Homeland Security (DHS)/Federal Emergency Management Agency (FEMA) in support of ESF #15 missions include:

- **Emergency Alert System (EAS):** The Federal Communications Commission (FCC) designed the EAS as a tool for the President to quickly send important emergency information to the Nation using radio, television, and cable systems. The EAS may also be used by State, tribal, and local authorities to deliver alerts and warnings. The EAS is required to deliver all EAS messages visually and aurally to be accessible to persons with hearing and vision disabilities.

- **Mobile Emergency Response Support (MERS):** DHS/FEMA MERS provides mobile telecommunications, operational support, life support, and power generation assets for the onsite management of all-hazard activities. MERS provides a deployable broadcast radio capability for multimedia communications, information processing, logistics, and operational support to Federal, State, and local authorities during incidents requiring a coordinated Federal response.

- **National Preparedness Network (PREPnet):** PREPnet is a DHS/FEMA television broadcast network capable of reaching large portions of the public in an impacted area with survival and recovery information before, during, and after catastrophic events. PREPnet delivers information via cable television, satellite services, personal digital devices, cell phones, and webcasts to both the public at large and to emergency responders. As a scalable DHS asset, PREPnet capabilities span a spectrum from simple public service announcements on up to 24/7 broadcast of recovery information to victims wherever they may have relocated.

- **Recovery Radio Support:** When commercial broadcast is impaired in an area, DHS/FEMA works with local broadcasters to set up Recovery Radio support, which provides official response and recovery information to local stations on an hourly basis through a pool feed. Distribution can be provided through the EAS network. All broadcasters are required to have equipment to monitor and air EAS programs, and most primary EAS stations have portable, remote pick-up equipment that can be installed in the Joint information Center (JIC).

ESF #15 – EXTERNAL AFFAIRS

MEMBERS

ESF Coordinator: Department of Homeland Security (DHS)

Primary Agency: Department of Homeland Security (DHS)/Federal Emergency Management Agency (FEMA)

Support Agencies: All

CONCEPT OF OPERATIONS OVERVIEW

ESF #15 integrates Public Affairs, Congressional Affairs, Intergovernmental Affairs (State, tribal, and local coordination), Community Relations, and the private sector under the coordinating auspices of External Affairs. The JIC ensures the coordinated release of information under ESF #15. The Planning and Products component of External Affairs develops all external and internal communications strategies and products for the ESF #15 organization.

ESF #15 provides the resources and structure for the implementation of the Incident Communications Emergency Policy and Procedures (ICEPP).

The DHS Assistant Secretary for Public Affairs, in coordination with the National Response Coordination Center (NRCC), activates and directs ESF #15 procedures.

The FEMA Office of Public Affairs designates a DHS/FEMA Public Affairs staff member as an ESF #15 representative to staff the NRCC as directed. When activated, ESF #15 activities are implemented in coordination with the DHS Office of Public Affairs (OPA) components of the National Operations Center and Domestic Readiness Group (DRG).

The staff of the DHS OPA coordinates messages with public affairs representatives from all involved departments and agencies.

ESF #15 provides the External Affairs Officer to the Joint Field Office Unified Coordination Staff who serves as the primary external affairs advisor to the Federal Coordinating Officer/Federal Resource Coordinator, Unified Coordination Group, and Principal Federal Official (PFO), if designated. ESF #15 may provide the same support to a National Special Security Event.

The External Affairs Officer reports to the ESF #15 Director and the Unified Coordination Group. The External Affairs Officer differs from a press secretary, which may be assigned to directly support a PFO, when designated.

To see the complete annex, as well as other pertinent information, refer to the NRF Resource Center at www.fema.gov/NRF.

Support Annex Summaries

Intentionally Left Blank

SUPPORT ANNEXES: INTRODUCTION

The Support Annexes describe how Federal departments and agencies; State, tribal, and local entities; the private sector; volunteer organizations; and nongovernmental organizations (NGOs) coordinate and execute the common functional processes and administrative requirements within the *National Response Framework* necessary to ensure efficient and effective incident management. During an incident, numerous procedures and administrative functions are required to support incident management.

The actions described in the Support Annexes are not limited to particular types of events but are overarching in nature and applicable to nearly every type of incident. In addition, they may support several or all Emergency Support Functions (ESFs). Examples include public affairs, international affairs, donations and volunteer management, and worker safety and health.

The Support Annexes may be fully or partially implemented without the Secretary of Homeland Security coordinating Federal operations.

The following section includes a series of annexes describing the roles and responsibilities of Federal departments and agencies, NGOs, and the private sector for those common activities that support the majority of incidents. The annexes address the following areas:

- Critical Infrastructure and Key Resources
- Financial Management
- International Coordination
- Private-Sector Coordination
- Public Affairs
- Tribal Relations
- Volunteer and Donations Management
- Worker Safety and Health

SUPPORT ANNEX MEMBER ROLES AND RESPONSIBILITIES

The overarching nature of functions described in these annexes frequently involves either the support to, or the cooperation of, all departments and agencies involved in incident management efforts to ensure seamless integration of and transitions between preparedness, response, and recovery activities.

Each annex is managed by one or more coordinating agencies and is supported by various cooperating agencies.

- **Coordinating Agency.** Federal agencies designated as coordinating agencies are responsible for implementation of processes detailed in the annexes. Coordinating agencies support the Department of Homeland Security (DHS) incident management mission by providing the leadership, expertise, and authorities to implement critical and specific aspects of the response.

- **Cooperating Agency.** Cooperating agencies are those entities that have specific expertise and capabilities to assist the coordinating agency in executing incident-related tasks or processes. When the procedures within a Support Annex are needed to support elements of an incident, the coordinating agency will notify cooperating agencies of the circumstances.

Intentionally Left Blank

CRITICAL INFRASTRUCTURE AND KEY RESOURCES

PURPOSE

The Critical Infrastructure and Key Resources Support Annex describes policies, roles and responsibilities, and the concept of operations for assessing, prioritizing, protecting, and restoring critical infrastructure and key resources (CIKR) of the United States and its territories and possessions during actual or potential domestic incidents. The annex details processes to ensure coordination and integration of CIKR-related activities among a wide array of public and private incident managers and CIKR security partners within immediate incident areas as well as at the regional and national levels.

SCOPE

This annex addresses integration of the CIKR protection[2] and restoration mission as a vital component of the Nation's unified approach to domestic incident management, which also may include CIKR-related international considerations.

Critical infrastructure includes those assets, systems, networks, and functions—physical or virtual—so vital to the United States that their incapacitation or destruction would have a debilitating impact on security, national economic security, public health or safety, or any combination of those matters. Key resources are publicly or privately controlled resources essential to minimal operation of the economy and the government.[3]

MEMBERS

Coordinating Agency: Department of Homeland Security (DHS)

Cooperating Agencies:
- Department of Agriculture
- Department of Commerce
- Department of Defense
- Department of Education
- Department of Energy
- Department of Health and Human Services
- Department of the Interior
- Department of Justice
- Department of Labor
- Department of State
- Department of Transportation
- Department of the Treasury
- Department of Veterans Affairs
- Environmental Protection Agency
- Federal Energy Regulatory Commission
- Nuclear Regulatory Commission
- Intelligence Community
- Office of Science and Technology Policy
- U.S. Postal Service
- Information Sharing and Analysis Center Council
- Partnership for Critical Infrastructure Security
- State, Local, Tribal, and Territorial Government Coordinating Council

---

[2] *National Infrastructure Protection Plan (NIPP)*, 2006, Glossary, pg. 104, defines the term *protection* as "actions to mitigate the overall risk to CIKR assets, systems, networks, or their interconnecting links resulting from exposure, injury, destruction, incapacitation, or exploitation. In the context of the *NIPP*, protection includes actions to deter the threat, mitigate vulnerabilities, or minimize consequences associated with a terrorist attack or other incident. Protection can include a wide range of activities, such as hardening facilities, building resiliency and redundancy, incorporating hazard resistance into initial facility design, initiating active or passive countermeasures, installing security systems, promoting workforce surety, and implementing cyber security measures, among various others."

[3] *NIPP*, 2006, Glossary of Key Terms, is the source for the definitions of critical infrastructure and key resources. These definitions are derived from the provisions of the Homeland Security Act of 2002 and HSPD-7.

CRITICAL INFRASTRUCTURE AND KEY RESOURCES

CONCEPT OF OPERATIONS OVERVIEW

The annex describes specific organizational approaches, processes, coordinating structures, and incident-related actions required for the protection and restoration of CIKR assets, systems, networks, or functions within the impacted area and outside the impacted area at the local, regional, and national levels.

The processes described herein are detailed further in standard operating procedures, field guides, and other related guidance developed collaboratively by DHS and the cooperating agencies to this annex.

DHS is responsible for leading, integrating, and coordinating the overall national effort to enhance CIKR protection, including developing and implementing comprehensive, multitiered risk management programs and methodologies; developing cross-sector and cross-jurisdictional protection guidance and protocols; and recommending risk management and performance criteria and metrics within and across sectors.

Federal departments and agencies provide support consistent with their CIKR-related statutory or regulatory responsibilities or with their designated functions as Sector-Specific Agencies (SSAs), Emergency Support Function (ESF) primary or supporting agencies, or coordinating or cooperating agencies for other related *National Response Framework* Support or Incident Annexes.

SSAs focus on overarching CIKR protection, risk management, and information sharing by working collaboratively with Sector Coordinating Councils (SCCs), Government Coordinating Councils (GCCs), relevant Federal departments and agencies, State, local, and tribal governments, ESFs, CIKR owners and operators, sector-based information-sharing mechanisms, and other private-sector entities.

SSAs coordinate CIKR efforts within their sectors to deter threats, mitigate vulnerabilities, and minimize consequences of manmade and natural incidents. Sector-Specific Plans (SSPs) specify each sector's approach to the risk management and information-sharing components of incident management.

State, tribal, and local government entities establish security partnerships, facilitate information sharing, and enable planning and preparedness for CIKR protection within their jurisdictions. Tribal governments are responsible for public health, welfare, safety, CIKR protection, and continuity of essential services within their jurisdictions. Local governments usually are responsible for emergency services and first-level responses to CIKR incidents. In some sectors, local governments own and operate CIKR such as water, wastewater, and storm water systems and electric utilities, and are responsible for initial prevention, response, recovery, and emergency services provision.

Private-sector CIKR owners and operators are responsible at the corporate and individual facility levels for risk and incident management planning, security, and preparedness investments.

To see the complete annex, as well as other pertinent information, refer to the NRF Resource Center, www.fema.gov/NRF.

FINANCIAL MANAGEMENT

PURPOSE

The Financial Management Support Annex provides basic financial management guidance for all participants in *National Response Framework (NRF)* activities. This includes guidance for all Federal departments and agencies providing assistance for incidents requiring a coordinated Federal response. The financial management function is a component of Emergency Support Function (ESF) #5 – Emergency Management.

The processes and procedures described in this annex ensure that funds are provided expeditiously and that financial operations are conducted in accordance with established Federal law, policies, regulations, and standards.

SCOPE

As part of the Secretary of Homeland Security's responsibility to coordinate resources under Homeland Security Presidential Directive (HSPD) 5, this annex is applicable to Federal departments and agencies ("Federal agencies") participating and responding under the National Response Framework with assistance or relief as coordinated by the Department of Homeland Security (DHS)/Federal Emergency Management Agency (FEMA) in response to incidents requiring a coordinated Federal response.

MEMBERS

Coordinating Agencies:
Department of Homeland Security (DHS)/Federal Emergency Management Agency (FEMA) (Stafford Act declarations)
Federal agency requesting Federal-to-Federal support (non-Stafford Act declarations)

Cooperating Agencies: All

CONCEPT OF OPERATIONS OVERVIEW

Stafford Act Declarations

The President may direct any Federal agency pursuant to the authorities in sections 402, 403, and 502 of the Stafford Act.

The Disaster Relief Fund (DRF), appropriated to DHS/FEMA, is available for purposes of the Stafford Act. Reimbursement may be provided from the DRF for activities conducted pursuant to these sections.

The DRF is not available for activities not authorized by the Stafford Act, for activities undertaken under other authorities or agency missions, or for non-Stafford incidents requiring a coordinated Federal response.

DHS/FEMA may issue mission assignments to other Federal agencies to: 1) address a State's request for Federal assistance to meet unmet emergency needs; or 2) support overall Federal operations pursuant to, or in anticipation of, a Stafford Act declaration. The mission assignment is issued to an agency by using FEMA Form 90-129, Mission Assignment with, as applicable, funding, funding limitations, the requirements of the task(s) to be performed, completion date, and State cost-share requirements.

Non-Stafford Act Incidents

A Federal entity with primary responsibility and statutory authority for handling an incident (i.e., the requesting agency) that needs support or assistance beyond its normal operations may request DHS coordination and facilitation through the *NRF*.

Generally, the requesting agency provides funding for the incident consistent with provisions of the Economy Act, unless other statutory authorities exist.

Federal agencies participating in the *NRF* may request and provide Federal-to-Federal support by executing inter/intra-agency reimbursable agreements, in accordance with applicable authorities. Federal agencies providing mutual aid support may request reimbursement from the requesting agency for eligible expenditures. The Request for Federal-to-Federal Support form (see Attachment 3, Tab 1 of the annex) may be used as the Reimbursement Agreement form by Federal agencies requesting support.

To see the complete annex, as well as other pertinent information, refer to the NRF Resource Center, www.fema.gov/NRF.

INTERNATIONAL COORDINATION

PURPOSE

The International Coordination Support Annex provides guidance on carrying out responsibilities for international coordination in support of the Federal Government's response to a domestic incident with an international component.

SCOPE

The International Coordination Support Annex supplements the *National Response Framework (NRF)*. The role of the Department of State (DOS) within the *NRF* is to fully support Federal, State, tribal, and local authorities in effective incident management and preparedness planning. A domestic incident will have international and diplomatic impacts and implications that call for coordination and consultations with foreign governments and international organizations. An incident may also require direct bilateral and multilateral actions on foreign affairs issues related to the incident, for which DOS has independent and sole responsibility.

MEMBERS

Coordinating Agency: Department of State

Cooperating Agencies:
- Department of Agriculture
- Department of Commerce
- Department of Defense
- Department of Energy
- Department of Health and Human Services
- Department of Homeland Security
- Department of Justice
- Department of Transportation
- U.S. Agency for International Development
- Other Federal Agencies
- American Red Cross

CONCEPT OF OPERATIONS OVERVIEW

Actions in this annex fall into two main categories: domestic coordination and foreign coordination.

Domestic Coordination

- **Domestic Support and International Outreach.** DOS's Executive Secretariat and its Operations Center establish a DOS Task Force when domestic incidents have major international implications.

- **Domestic DOS Facilities/Personnel.** DOS coordinates with other Federal, State, tribal, or local authorities to respond to events at DOS domestic facilities and ensures the safety and security of DOS personnel.

- **Support to Foreign Missions/Foreign Nationals in the United States.**

  - Ensures (along with Federal, State, tribal, and local authorities) the protection of foreign missions, the U.N., and other multilateral organizations with missions in the United States, and for the safety/security of their official personnel.

  - Assists foreign Embassies/Consulates in coordinating with Federal, State, tribal, and local authorities to enable foreign diplomatic missions to provide information to their citizens in the United States and to render safety/security and other consular assistance.

Foreign Coordination

- **Immediate U.S. Government Incident Management – Operational Needs.** DOS coordinates U.S. Government communications with other nations, through Embassies/Consulates, regarding crisis response and other activities.

- **Provision of Information to Americans Abroad, Foreign Governments, and the International Community.**

  - Advises American citizens and businesses and other U.S. social/economic entities abroad of the nature and extent of the situation in the United States and any direct effect that the domestic incident might have on their safety and security.

  - Serves as a liaison between foreign governments and U.S. agencies on real-time actions taken or planned, and coordinates U.S. Government projections of longer term international consequences of the event.

  - Develops and implements a diplomatic and international public affairs and public diplomacy strategy in coordination with the National Response Coordination Center to communicate information concerning the status of the incident and highlight U.S. and international response and mitigation efforts.

DOS as Intermediary for Requests/Offers of Assistance

  - Coordinates requests for foreign assistance based on needs conveyed by DHS or other Federal agencies.

  - Acts as the formal diplomatic mechanism for handling U.S. Government requests to other nations for assistance in meeting additional, ongoing U.S. response needs.

  - Acts as the intermediary for foreign offers of assistance to the U.S. Government. Works with U.S. Government departments and agencies to respond appropriately to such requests.

NOTE: The International Assistance System (IAS) Concept of Operations details the procedures for conveying information on needs to the international community, requesting foreign assistance, and reviewing offers of foreign assistance.

To see the complete annex, as well as other pertinent information, refer to the NRF Resource Center, www.fema.gov/NRF.

PRIVATE-SECTOR COORDINATION

PURPOSE

The Private-Sector Coordination Support Annex describes the policies, responsibilities, and concept of operations for Federal incident management activities involving the private sector during incidents requiring a coordinated Federal response. In this context, the annex further describes the activities necessary to ensure effective coordination and integration with the private sector, both for-profit and not-for-profit, including the Nation's critical infrastructure, key resources, other business and industry components, and not-for-profit organizations (sometimes called nongovernmental organizations (NGOs)), including those serving special needs populations, engaged in response and recovery. The Critical Infrastructure and Key Resources (CIKR) Support Annex focuses on the CIKR efforts of the private sector while this annex focuses on the remaining portion of the private sector.

SCOPE

This annex applies to all Federal executive agencies operating under the *National Response Framework (NRF)* in incidents requiring a coordinated Federal response that involve the private sector in any of the following ways:

- Impacted organization or infrastructure
- Response resource
- Regulated and/or responsible party
- Member of the State emergency management organization

MEMBERS

Coordinating Agency: Department of Homeland Security (DHS)

Cooperating Agencies: All

CONCEPT OF OPERATIONS OVERVIEW

Department of Homeland Security: In the event of a potential or actual incident, the DHS Office of the Secretary coordinates strategic communications with CEOs, senior officials, or individuals specifically designated by these private-sector leaders to engage in such communications on their behalf.

Further, the Secretary of Homeland Security utilizes a private-sector advisory group with representatives from across the spectrum of CIKR, business, and industry, as well as not-for-profit organizations, to provide advice on incident management and emergency response issues affecting their constituencies.

Private Sector Office (DHS/PSO): The DHS/PSO encourages private-sector preparedness for incident management by:

- Identifying and promoting security and preparedness activities in national preparedness, prevention, response, and recovery.
- Promoting educational efforts to prepare for natural disasters or terrorist incidents.
- Encouraging the identification and sharing of best practices through promoting use of consensus standards and best practices.

PRIVATE-SECTOR COORDINATION

DHS/PSO provides representatives to the National Operations Center (NOC) components as required, and to the Joint Field Office (JFO) to enable strategic coordination with the private sector during incidents requiring a coordinated Federal response.

Office of Infrastructure Protection (DHS/OIP): DHS/OIP supports prevention, preparedness, response, and recovery efforts involving CIKR, in accordance with Homeland Security Presidential Directive 7, Critical Infrastructure, Identification, Prioritization, and Protection (HSPD-7), and other private-sector entities as appropriate, through facilitating and coordinating protection and response planning, procedures, and exercises. DHS/OIP implements the programmatic policy and strategy for information sharing.

National Infrastructure Coordinating Center (NICC): The NICC monitors the Nation's CIKR on a 24/7 basis and provides a mechanism and process to share and exchange information with the private sector and the HSPD-7 SSAs.

Sector-Specific Agencies (SSA): SSAs, as designated in HSPD-7, focus on overarching CIKR protection, risk management, and information sharing by working collaboratively with relevant Federal departments and agencies; State, tribal, and local governments; CIKR owners and operators; and other private-sector entities.

Private-sector for-profit and not-for-profit organizations: These groups, like Federal, State, tribal, and local governmental organizations, report threats, incidents, and potential incidents to the NOC using existing jurisdictional incident reporting mechanisms and reporting channels. The NOC receives threat and operational information regarding incidents or potential incidents from these organizations and jurisdictions and makes an initial determination to initiate the coordination of Federal incident management activities.

To see the complete annex, as well as other pertinent information, refer to the NRF Resource Center, www.fema.gov/NRF.

PUBLIC AFFAIRS

PURPOSE

The Public Affairs Support Annex describes the interagency policies and procedures used to rapidly mobilize Federal assets to prepare and deliver coordinated and sustained messages to the public in response to incidents requiring a coordinated Federal response.

SCOPE

As part of the Secretary of Homeland Security's responsibility to coordinate incident management under Homeland Security Presidential Directive 5, the *National Response Framework (NRF)* Incident Communications Emergency Policy and Procedures (ICEPP) provides detailed guidance to Federal incident communicators on activities to be initiated in conjunction with incidents requiring a coordinated Federal response. It is applicable to all Federal departments and agencies responding under the *NRF*. It establishes mechanisms to prepare and deliver coordinated and sustained messages regarding incidents requiring a coordinated Federal response, and provides for prompt Federal acknowledgement of an incident and communication of emergency information to the public during incident management operations.

The ICEPP is comprised of two annexes contained in the *NRF*:

- Public Affairs Support Annex: Describes the interagency policies and procedures for incident communications with the public.

- ESF #15 – External Affairs Annex: Outlines the functions, resources, and capabilities for external affairs.

Additionally, the ESF #15 Standard Operating Procedures (SOP) exist within the parameters established by the *NRF*. The SOP establishes specific procedures and protocols for ESF #15 to support Federal domestic incident management during an incident requiring a coordinated Federal response.

The policies outlined in all of these documents are based on, and flow through, the *NRF*, the *National Incident Management System (NIMS)*, and the ESF #15 SOP, which further outlines the guidance, protocols, and tactics of the Joint Information System (JIS), the Incident Command System (ICS), and Federal external affairs actions. All of these elements are integrated with and supported through the ESF #15 resource management structure.

MEMBERS

Coordinating Agency: Department of Homeland Security (DHS)

Cooperating Agencies: All

PUBLIC AFFAIRS

CONCEPT OF OPERATIONS OVERVIEW

During an incident, Federal, State, tribal, and local authorities share responsibility for communicating information regarding the incident to the public. These actions are a critical component of incident management and must be fully integrated with all other operational actions to ensure the following objectives are met:

- Delivery of incident preparedness, health, response, and recovery instructions to those directly affected by the incident.
- Dissemination of incident information to the public, including special needs populations.

The Joint Information Center (JIC) structure provides a supporting mechanism to develop, coordinate, and deliver messages. It supports the Incident Commander or Unified Command and the associated elements of the ICS.

A Federal core group develops, coordinates, and delivers information and instructions to the public related to:

- Federal assistance to the incident-affected area.
- Federal departmental/agency response.
- National preparations.
- Protective measures.
- Impact on nonaffected areas.
- Federal law enforcement activities.

Assignments to this core group are determined by the DHS Office of Public Affairs (OPA) in accordance with jurisdictional and statutory responsibilities, operational tasks, areas of expertise and responsibility, and the nature and location of the incident.

The DHS OPA has primary responsibility for coordinating the Federal incident communications effort by:

- Providing a leadership role during domestic incidents when significant interagency coordination is required.
- Identifying Federal department and interagency participants, and arranging conference calls and other activities necessary for ESF #15 coordination.
- Establishing a strategic communications flow during an incident requiring a coordinated Federal response.
- Designating an ESF #15 team comprised of external affairs officials from various Federal Government departments and agencies.
- Providing coordination with the Homeland Security Council (HSC) and other entities within the Executive Office of the President on matters related to dissemination of incident-related information to the public.

To see the complete annex, as well as other pertinent information, refer to the NRF Resource Center, www.fema.gov/NRF.

TRIBAL RELATIONS

PURPOSE

The Tribal Relations Support Annex describes the policies, responsibilities, and concept of operations for effective coordination and interaction of Federal incident management activities with those of tribal governments and communities during incidents requiring a coordinated Federal response. The processes and functions described in this annex help facilitate the delivery of incident management programs, resources, and support to tribal governments and individuals.

SCOPE

This annex applies to all Federal departments and agencies working under the *National Response Framework (NRF)* in response to incidents requiring Federal coordination, including tribes recognized by the Federal Government.

Because tribal governments are fully integrated into the *NRF*, this annex addresses only those factors in the relationship between Federal departments and agencies and the federally recognized tribes.

The guidance provided in this annex does not contravene existing laws governing Federal relationships with federally recognized tribes.

MEMBERS

Coordinating Agency: Department of Homeland Security (DHS)

Cooperating Agencies:
- Department of Agriculture
- Department of Health and Human Services
- Department of the Interior
- All Others

CONCEPT OF OPERATIONS OVERVIEW

State Governors must request a Presidential disaster declaration on behalf of a tribe under the Stafford Act. However, Federal departments and agencies can work directly with tribes within existing agency authorities and resources in the absence of such a declaration.

Tribal relations functions, resources, and liaison operations are coordinated through Emergency Support Function (ESF) #15 – External Affairs.

A Tribal Relations Element is established in the Joint Field Office (JFO) to provide the operational capability for collecting and sharing relevant incident information, alerting and deploying required tribal relations staff to or near the affected area, and ensuring compliance with Federal laws relating to tribal relations.

For incidents that directly impact tribal jurisdictions, a tribal representative shall be included in the Unified Coordination Group, as required.

TRIBAL RELATIONS

A tribe may appoint a member of the tribe to serve as a tribal liaison in the JFO. As authorized by the tribal government, the tribal liaison:

- Is responsible for coordinating tribal resources needed to prevent, respond to, and recover from incidents of all types. This also includes preparedness and mitigation activities.

- May have powers to amend or suspend certain tribal laws or ordinances associated with response.

- Communicates with the tribal community and helps people, businesses, and organizations cope with the consequences of any type of incident.

- Negotiates mutual aid and assistance agreements with other tribes or jurisdictions.

- Can request Federal assistance under the Stafford Act through the Governor of the State when it becomes clear that the tribe's capabilities will be insufficient or have been exceeded.

- Elect to deal directly with the Federal Government. Although a State Governor must request a Presidential disaster declaration on behalf of a tribe under the Stafford Act, Federal departments or agencies can work directly with the tribe within existing authorities and resources.

To see the complete annex, as well as other pertinent information, refer to the NRF Resource Center, www.fema.gov/NRF.

VOLUNTEER AND DONATIONS MANAGEMENT

PURPOSE

The Volunteer and Donations Management Support Annex describes the coordination processes used to support the State in ensuring the most efficient and effective use of unaffiliated volunteers, unaffiliated organizations, and unsolicited donated goods to support all Emergency Support Functions (ESFs) for incidents requiring a Federal response, including offers of unaffiliated volunteer services and unsolicited donations to the Federal Government.

SCOPE

This annex provides guidance on the Federal role in supporting State governments in the management of masses of unaffiliated volunteers and unsolicited donated goods. (Any reference to volunteer services and donated goods in this annex refers to unaffiliated volunteer services[4] and unsolicited goods, unless otherwise stated.) This guidance applies to all agencies and organizations with direct and indirect volunteer and/or donations responsibilities under the *National Response Framework*.

MEMBERS

ESF Coordinator: Department of Homeland Security (DHS)/Federal Emergency Management Agency (FEMA)

Cooperating Agencies:
- Department of Agriculture
- Department of Health and Human Services
- Department of Homeland Security
- Department of State
- Department of Transportation
- Corporation for National and Community Service
- General Services Administration
- U.S. Agency for International Development
- USA Freedom Corps
- National Voluntary Organizations Active in Disaster

---

[4] Unaffiliated volunteers, also known as spontaneous volunteers, are individuals who offer to help or self-deploy to assist in emergency situations without fully coordinating their activities. They are considered "unaffiliated" in that they are not part of a disaster relief organization. Although unaffiliated volunteers can be significant resources, because they do not have preestablished relationships with emergency response organizations, verifying their training or credentials and matching them with the appropriate service areas can be difficult.

VOLUNTEER AND DONATIONS MANAGEMENT

CONCEPT OF OPERATIONS OVERVIEW

The Federal Government supports State and tribal government efforts to manage unaffiliated volunteers and unsolicited donated goods. Requests for support under this annex from Federal, State, tribal, and local authorities generally are coordinated through the Regional Response Coordination Center (RRCC) or the Joint Field Office (JFO). Depending on the situation, however, coordination may occur at the National Response Coordination Center (NRCC). DHS/FEMA provides Volunteer and Donations Management staff to the NRCC, RRCC, and JFO in support of the State, as required.

Federal support of volunteer and donations management operations may include:

- Activation of a Volunteer/Donations Coordination Team at DHS/FEMA Headquarters to expedite service provided to donors from large private-sector entities, large civic organizations, and others, and to address large national media-driven collection drives and other complex situations involving donated goods and volunteer services.

- At the request of the State or tribal government, a national donations and volunteer management Web-based application that enables the general public to register their offers of donated goods and services, thus providing the State/tribal Volunteer/Donations Coordination Team a real-time view of offers and the ability to match offers to needs.

- Coordination with appropriate DHS/FEMA Divisions/Offices, the Corporation for National and Community Service (CNCS), National Voluntary Organizations Active in Disaster (National VOAD) leadership, the Points of Light & Hands On Network leadership and their Volunteer Centers, State VOAD leadership, and other stakeholders as necessary.

- Facilities management such as multiagency warehouse and volunteer reception center capabilities.

- Communications support such as coordination of a national hotline and/or call center.

The CNCS supports utilization of volunteers who are not part of the preexisting Federal, State, tribal, and/or local emergency management structure.

National VOAD supports the management of unsolicited donations including efforts to maximize the utility of unsolicited donations, public information campaigns, and disposition of unneeded goods.

To see the complete annex, as well as other pertinent information, refer to the NRF Resource Center, www.fema.gov/NRF.

WORKER SAFETY AND HEALTH

PURPOSE

The Worker Safety and Health Support Annex provides Federal support to Federal, State, tribal, and local response and recovery worker safety and health during incidents requiring a coordinated Federal response. The annex, coordinated by the Department of Labor (DOL)/Occupational Safety and Health Administration (OSHA), describes the technical assistance resources, capabilities, and other support to ensure that response and recovery worker safety and health risks are anticipated, recognized, evaluated, communicated, and consistently controlled.

SCOPE

This annex describes the technical assistance resources, capabilities, and other support to ensure that response and recovery worker safety and health risks are anticipated, recognized, evaluated, communicated, and consistently controlled. This annex addresses the coordination and provision of technical assistance for worker safety and health management activities; it does not address public health and safety. It also describes coordination mechanisms, policies, and processes to provide technical assistance for incident response and recovery worker safety and health management activities that include anticipation, identification, and mitigation of incident response and recovery of risks and hazards.

This annex is structured to provide technical assistance and support for response and recovery worker safety and health in the changing requirements of domestic incident management to include preparedness, prevention, response, and recovery actions. Activities within the scope of this function include development of health and safety plans; identifying, assessing, and controlling health and safety hazards; conducting response and recovery exposure monitoring; collecting and managing data; providing technical assistance and support for personal protective equipment programs, incident-specific response and recovery worker training, and medical surveillance; providing exposure and risk management information; and providing technical assistance to include industrial hygiene expertise, occupational safety and health expertise, engineering expertise, and occupational medicine expertise.

MEMBERS

Coordinating Agency: Department of Labor (DOL)/Occupational Safety and Health Administration (OSHA)

Cooperating Agencies:
- Department of Defense
- Department of Energy
- Department of Health and Human Services
- Department of Homeland Security
- Environmental Protection Agency

WORKER SAFETY AND HEALTH

CONCEPT OF OPERATIONS OVERVIEW

When implemented, this annex will coordinate with Federal, State, tribal, local, and if necessary, private-sector officials to determine potential needs for worker safety and health support.

At the Federal Headquarters-level, this annex operates under the direction and leadership of the Assistant Secretary for Occupational Safety and Health.

The DOL/OSHA Regional Administrator provides staff to coordinate the provision of support activities for this annex at the Regional Response Coordination Center (RRCC) and the Joint Field Office (JFO). Within the JFO, the Department of Homeland Security (DHS)/Federal Emergency Management Agency (FEMA) Disaster Safety Officer (DSO) ensures that the Federal Coordinating Officer (FCO) receives accurate and timely safety and health information and technical assistance to ensure the safety of the FEMA staff and personnel in the JFO and other FEMA-managed facilities.

The coordinator for this annex ensures the FCO, the Unified Coordination Group, and the Chief of Staff have consistent, accurate, and timely worker safety and health information for theatre-wide operations, and coordinates the delivery of Federal worker safety and health technical assistance and resources to Federal, State, tribal, and local responders. The coordinator for this annex convenes and chairs the JFO's Interagency Safety and Health Committee. This committee is made up of representatives from the various agencies (including Federal, State, tribal, and local response organizations) within the JFO and coordinates the worker safety and health program among the various agencies.

When activated, both the FEMA DSO and the coordinator for this annex make up the safety function on the JFO Coordination Staff. Further, when implemented, this annex will be represented within the Operations and Planning Sections of the JFO. Additionally, staff of this annex may serve as technical specialists in other JFO elements as required.

The support provided through the Worker Safety and Health Support Annex will be dependent upon the scope, complexity, and specific hazards associated with the incident and the needs of the response and recovery organizations. Specific requests for assistance will be coordinated by DHS/FEMA and defined in mission assignments.

The following describes general functional support that can be provided under this annex:

- Worker Safety and Health Needs Assessment
- Health and Safety Plans
- Safety and Health Assessment
- Personal Protective Equipment
- Data Management
- Training and Communication
- Response and Recovery Worker Health and Medical Surveillance

---

To see the complete annex, as well as other pertinent information, refer to the NRF Resource Center, www.fema.gov/NRF.

---

www.ingramcontent.com/pod-product-compliance
Lightning Source LLC
Chambersburg PA
CBHW080532290526

45790CB00006B/2382